GREEN BAY PACKERS

BY BRIAN HOWELL

The Child's World

Published by The Child's World®
1980 Lookout Drive • Mankato, MN 56003-1705
800-599-READ • www.childsworld.com

Acknowledgments
The Child's World®: Mary Berendes, Publishing Director
Red Line Editorial: Editorial direction
The Design Lab: Design
Amnet: Production

Design Element: Dean Bertoncelj/Shutterstock Images
Photographs ©: Photographs ©: David Stluka/AP Images,
cover; Chris O'Meara/AP Images, 5; Allen Fredrickson/
Icon Sportswire, 7; Vernon Biever/NFL Photo/AP Images, 9;
John Ehlke/West Bend Daily News/AP Images, 11;
Shutterstock Images, 13; Scott Boehm/AP Images, 14-15;
AP Images, 17; Jeffrey Phelps/AP Images, 19; 239/AP
Images, 21; Vernon Biever/AP Images, 23; Mike Roemer/AP
Images, 25; Matt Ludtke/AP Images, 27; John Sommers/
Icon Sportswire, 29

ISBN 9781634070096
LCCN 2014959714

Printed in the United States of America
Mankato, MN
July, 2015
PA02265

ABOUT THE AUTHOR

Brian Howell is a freelance writer based in Denver, Colorado. He has been a sports journalist for nearly 20 years and has written dozens of books about sports and two about American history. A native of Colorado, he lives with his wife and four children in his home state.

TABLE OF CONTENTS

GO, PACKERS! 4

WHO ARE THE PACKERS? 6

WHERE THEY CAME FROM 8

WHO THEY PLAY 10

WHERE THEY PLAY 12

THE FOOTBALL FIELD 14

BIG DAYS 16

TOUGH DAYS 18

MEET THE FANS 20

HEROES THEN 22

HEROES NOW 24

GEARING UP 26

SPORTS STATS 28

GLOSSARY 30

FIND OUT MORE 31

INDEX 32

GO, PACKERS!

The Green Bay Packers have won a lot of big games. They have won 13 professional football championships. That is more than any other team. Four of those championships have been **Super Bowl** wins. Green Bay has more than 20 players in the **Hall of Fame**. The Packers also had legendary coach Vince Lombardi. The Super Bowl trophy is named after him. The Packers have been thrilling their fans for more than 90 years. Let's meet the Packers.

Quarterback Aaron Rodgers (right) and linebacker Clay Matthews celebrate after Green Bay's 31–25 Super Bowl win over the Pittsburgh Steelers on February 6, 2011.

WHO ARE THE PACKERS?

The Green Bay Packers play in the National Football **League** (NFL). They are one of the 32 teams in the NFL. The NFL includes the American Football Conference (AFC) and the National Football Conference (NFC). The winner of the NFC plays the winner of the AFC in the Super Bowl. The Packers play in the North Division of the NFC. The Packers won the Super Bowl after the 1966, 1967, 1996, and 2010 seasons. They also won nine NFL Championships before the Super Bowl began after the 1966 season.

Quarterback Brett Favre ranks in the top two in NFL history in career passing yards and passing touchdowns.

WHERE THEY CAME FROM

It was late summer in 1919. The Indian Packing Company in Green Bay, Wisconsin, wanted to start a new football team. The team would be called the Packers. Curly Lambeau was an Indian Packing Company employee. He was named team captain. The team was mostly former players from local high schools. The Packers joined the American Professional Football Association (APFA) in 1921. The APFA later became the NFL.

The Super Bowl trophy is named after legendary Packers coach Vince Lombardi.

WHO THEY PLAY

The Green Bay Packers play 16 games each season. With so few games, each one is important. Every year, the Packers play two games against each of the other three teams in their division. Those teams are the Chicago Bears, Detroit Lions, and Minnesota Vikings. The Packers also play six other teams from the NFC and four from the AFC. The Packers and Bears are the NFL's oldest **rivals**. They have been playing each other since 1921.

Linebacker Clay Matthews sacks Bears quarterback Jay Cutler in a 55-14 Green Bay win on November 9, 2014.

WHERE THEY PLAY

The Packers play at historic Lambeau Field. It opened in 1957. The only professional sports teams that have played in their current homes longer are baseball's Chicago Cubs and Boston Red Sox. Lambeau Field was originally called City Stadium. Curly Lambeau died in 1965. The stadium was renamed in his honor. Lambeau Field has had several upgrades. It held about 32,000 fans at first. Now nearly 81,000 fans fill the stadium on game days.

Lambeau Field is one of the most iconic stadiums in American sports.

THE FOOTBALL FIELD

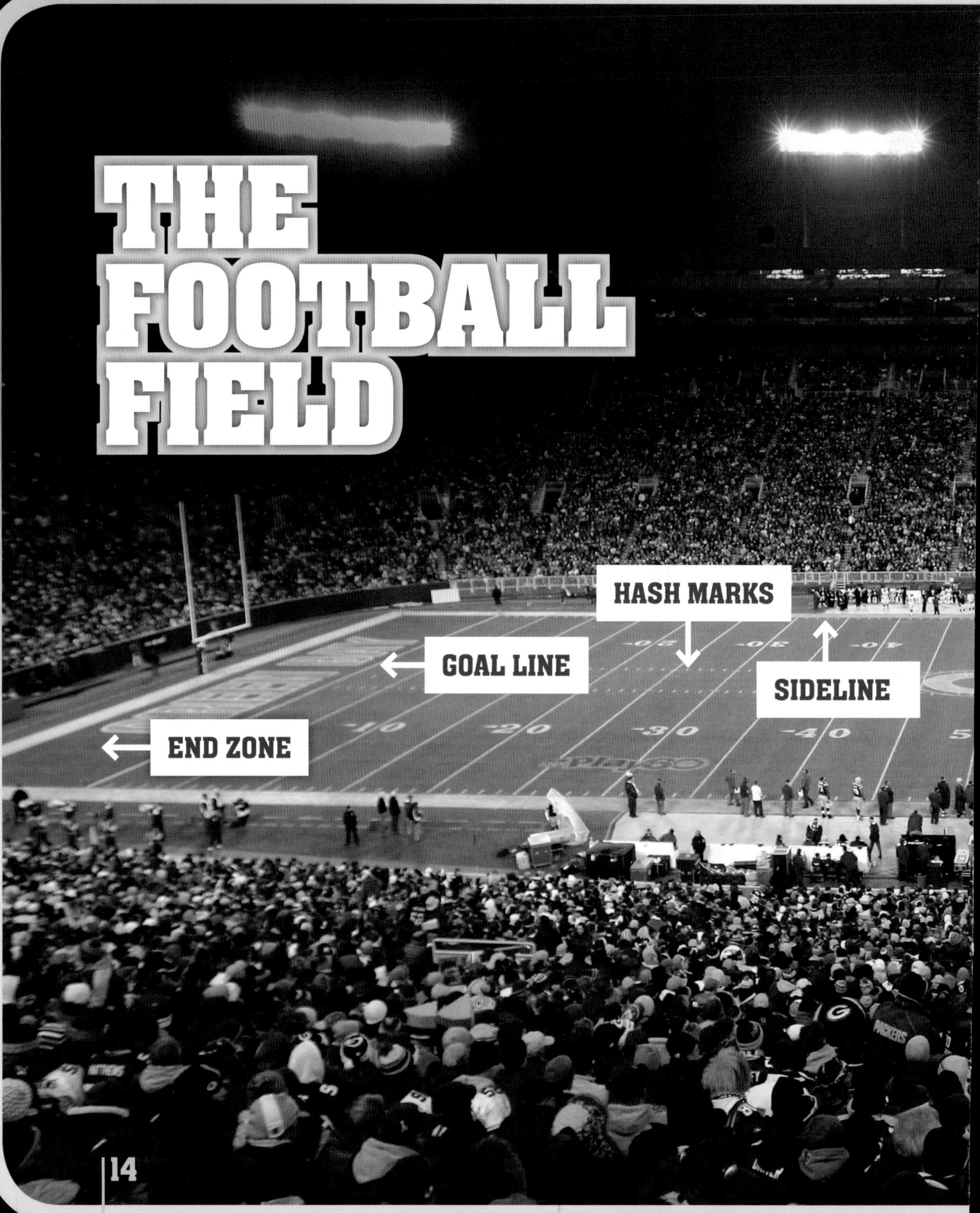

HASH MARKS

GOAL LINE

SIDELINE

END ZONE

GOAL POST →

BENCH AREA

← MIDFIELD

END LINE →

20-YARD LINE

BIG DAYS

The Packers have had some great moments in their history. Here are three of the greatest:

1929—The Packers won their first NFL Championship. They went 12-0-1. Green Bay allowed just 22 points all season. It was the first of three consecutive NFL Championships for the Packers.

1967—On December 31, the Packers played the Dallas Cowboys in the NFL Championship Game. It was minus-15°F (minus-26°C) at Lambeau Field. The game was nicknamed "The Ice Bowl." Green Bay won 21-17. The Packers then defeated the Oakland Raiders two weeks later in the second Super Bowl.

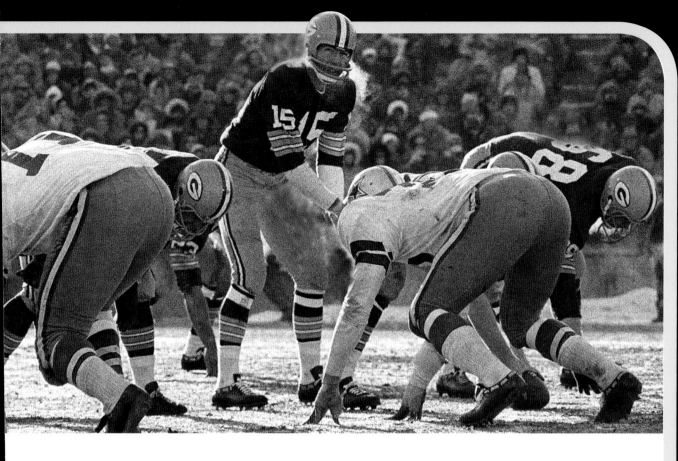

Quarterback Bart Starr gets ready to take a snap during "The Ice Bowl," which the Packers won 21–17 against the Dallas Cowboys on December 31, 1967.

1996—Green Bay had not won a title in 29 years. But quarterback Brett Favre changed that. The 1996 Packers won the Super Bowl on January 26, 1997. Favre threw for two touchdowns. He also rushed for one. Green Bay beat the New England Patriots 35–21.

TOUGH DAYS

Football is a hard game. Even the best teams have rough games and seasons. Here are some of the toughest times in Packers history:

1958—This was the worst season in Packers history. They finished 1-10-1. Green Bay missed the **playoffs** for the 14th straight year.

1963—Paul Hornung was a Green Bay fan favorite. His nickname was "The Golden Boy." He was the NFL **Most Valuable Player (MVP)** in 1961. But he was caught betting on NFL games. That is against the rules. He was suspended the entire season.

2009—Brett Favre is one of the best quarterbacks ever. He is a Packers legend. But he left the team. Favre

Quarterback Brett Favre salutes the crowd after returning to Lambeau Field with the Minnesota Vikings and beating the Packers 38–26 on November 1, 2009.

played for the New York Jets in 2008 before joining the rival Minnesota Vikings in 2009. His first game back in Green Bay was on November 1. Fans booed him. Minnesota's 38–26 win made it even worse.

MEET THE FANS

Packers fans are nicknamed "Cheeseheads." Many of them wear foam blocks that look like cheese on their heads to games. Players jump into the stands after scoring touchdowns. It is called "The Lambeau Leap." Green Bay fans have a unique relationship with their team. Many of them own small parts of the Packers. Most NFL teams have one owner or a small group of owners. But not the Packers. The public has owned the Packers through **stock** since 1923. More than 360,000 fans own a small share of the team.

Green Bay fans are known around football for wearing foam pieces of headgear shaped like cheese.

HEROES THEN

Vince Lombardi coached Green Bay from 1959 to 1967. He is one of the best football leaders of all time. The Packers won five NFL Championships under him. Bart Starr quarterbacked those teams. Starr, Paul Hornung, and Jim Taylor were all NFL MVPs in the 1960s. Linebacker Ray Nitschke was a defensive star from 1958 to 1972. Defensive end Reggie White also shined with the Packers. He played in Green Bay from 1993 to 1998. White was the 1998 NFL Defensive Player of the Year. Quarterback Brett Favre had a rocket arm. He was known for taking risks. He was also one of the NFL's greatest quarterbacks. He played with Green Bay from 1992 to 2007. Favre was named NFL MVP in 1995 and 1996. He shared the award with Detroit Lions running back Barry Sanders in 1997.

Paul Hornung played halfback, fullback, kicker, and quarterback for the Packers.

HEROES NOW

Aaron Rodgers took over at quarterback in 2008. He is now the team's most popular player. Rodgers is on his way to becoming an all-time great. He led Green Bay to a Super Bowl title after the 2010 season. Rodgers was the NFL MVP in 2011. He passed for 4,643 yards and 45 touchdowns that year. He won the award again in 2014. Rodgers has talented receivers on his side. Randall Cobb and Jordy Nelson make it hard on defenses every week. Packers fans also love linebacker Clay Matthews. His father and uncle both played in the NFL. But Clay has made a name for himself. He made the **Pro Bowl** in each of his first four seasons from 2009 to 2012.

Wide receiver Randall Cobb does "The Lambeau Leap" after scoring a touchdown against the Jacksonville Jaguars on October 28, 2012.

GEARING UP

NFL players wear team uniforms. They wear helmets and pads to keep them safe. Cleats help them make quick moves and run fast. Some players wear extra gear for protection.

THE FOOTBALL

NFL footballs are made of leather. Under the leather is a lining that fills with air to give the ball its shape. The leather has bumps or "pebbles." These help players grip the ball. Laces help players control their throws. Footballs are also called "pigskins" because some of the first balls were made from pig bladders. Today they are made of leather from cows.

Running back Eddie Lacy was the 2013 NFL Offensive Rookie of the Year.

HELMET

SHOULDER PADS

GLOVES

THIGH PADS

FOOTBALL

SPORTS STATS

Here are some of the all-time career records for the Green Bay Packers. All the stats are through the 2014 season.

PASSING YARDS

Brett Favre 61,655

Aaron Rodgers 28,578

RUSHING YARDS

Ahman Green 8,322

Jim Taylor 8,207

TOTAL TOUCHDOWNS

Don Hutson 105

Jim Taylor 91

INTERCEPTIONS

Bobby Dillon 52

Willie Wood 48

SACKS

Kabeer Gbaja-Biamila 74.5

Reggie White 68.5

POINTS

Ryan Longwell 1,054

Mason Crosby 1,037

Wide receiver Donald Driver made the Pro Bowl three times during his 14-year career with the Packers.

RECEPTIONS

Donald Driver 743
Sterling Sharpe 595

GLOSSARY

Hall of Fame a museum in Canton, Ohio, that honors the best players

league an organization of sports teams that compete against each other

Most Valuable Player (MVP) a yearly award given to the top player in the NFL

playoffs a series of games after the regular season that decides which two teams play in the Super Bowl

Pro Bowl the NFL's All-Star game, in which the best players in the league compete

rivals teams whose games bring out the greatest emotion between the players and the fans on both sides

stock shares, or a small piece of ownership, of a team or company

Super Bowl the championship game of the NFL, played between the winners of the AFC and the NFC

FIND OUT MORE

IN THE LIBRARY

Editors of Sports Illustrated Kids. *Sports Illustrated Kids Football: Then to WOW!* New York: Sports Illustrated, 2014.

Frisch, Aaron. *Super Bowl Champions: Green Bay Packers.* Mankato, MN: Creative Paperbacks, 2014.

Green, David, and Mary Tiegreen. *101 Reasons to Love the Packers.* New York: Stewart, Tabori and Chang, 2012.

ON THE WEB

Visit our Web site for links about the Green Bay Packers:
childsworld.com/links

Note to Parents, Teachers, and Librarians: We routinely verify our Web links to make sure they are safe and active sites. So encourage your readers to check them out!

INDEX

American Football
    Conference (AFC), 6, 10
American Professional
    Football Association
    (APFA), 8

Chicago Bears, 10
Cobb, Randall, 24

Dallas Cowboys, 16
Detroit Lions, 10, 22

Favre, Brett, 17, 18, 22

Hornung, Paul, 18, 22

"Ice Bowl, The," 16

Lambeau, Curly, 8, 12
Lambeau Field, 12, 16
"Lambeau Leap, The," 20
Lombardi, Vince, 4, 22

Matthews, Clay, 24
Minnesota Vikings, 10, 19

National Football Conference
    (NFC), 6, 10
National Football League
    (NFL), 6, 8, 10, 16, 18, 20, 22,
    24, 26
Nelson, Jordy, 24
New England Patriots, 17
New York Jets, 19
NFC North, 6, 10
NFL Championship, 6, 16
Nitschke, Ray, 22

Oakland Raiders, 16

Rodgers, Aaron, 24

Sanders, Barry, 22
Starr, Bart, 22
Super Bowl, 4, 6, 16, 17, 24

Taylor, Jim, 22

White, Reggie, 22